THE
READING
HOUSE

This book belongs to:

Text copyright © 2022 Caterpillar Books Ltd.
Cover art and interior illustrations copyright © 2021, 2022 by WeDoo Studio
All rights reserved. Published in the United States by The Reading House,
an imprint of Random House Children's Books, a division of
Penguin Random House LLC, New York. The Reading House and
the colophon are registered trademarks of Penguin Random House LLC.
rhcbooks.com
Educators and librarians, for a variety of teaching tools,
visit us at RHTeachersLibrarians.com
ISBN: 978-0-593-51617-1
Printed in China
10 9 8 7 6 5 4 3 2 1
First North American Edition
CPB/1800/2032/1121

Kindergarten
Reading and Writing

Contents

This is going to be **fun**!

Welcome to The Reading House

Marla Conn, MS Ed., is a reading and literacy specialist with a Master of Science in Elementary Education and Reading, and over 15 years of experience as a teacher in New York public schools.

During my years as a teacher, literacy specialist, and educational consultant, I have worked with hundreds of children and have a deep understanding of how the right books and instructional materials can provide rich, meaningful experiences that build a strong foundation for learning.

The Reading House was created out of the need to provide children with a comprehensive and systematic educational tool. It combines dependable strategies that have been proven to motivate, educate, and spark the process of learning, using an innovative storybook, character-based approach.

What began as a leveled learn-to-read program has grown into an entire educational universe, with materials to cover all aspects of early learning, in a variety of engaging formats. Each book in the series has been carefully devised and designed to inspire and encourage young children and adheres to the core principles and key building blocks of early learning.

The Reading House is one-of-a-kind: an inviting, accessible, informative space where children can learn and grow. With its engaging cast of characters, bright and playful illustrations, and consistent setting, The Reading House is a world that early learners will love to return to, again and again.

I am so excited for children to get their hands on these books and to watch the lightbulbs switch on!

Happy Reading!
Marla Conn

Let's get **started!**

Hints and Tips for Parents and Guardians

Kindergarten Reading and Writing supports kindergarteners in the development of the key literacy skills they will need to be school-ready. Designed to be as enjoyable as it is educational, little learners are joined on their journey by the fantastically fun cast of The Reading House.

The activities in this workbook build upon the basic preschool concepts learned in **My First Writing Skills**, introducing children to a more complex set of skills, including phonics and word structure, sentence-building, and basic comprehension. This workbook is the perfect companion for readying learners for their school ventures.

Before embarking on this exciting journey, there are a few hints and tips parents and guardians should bear in mind.

★ BUILD SKILLS:

This workbook is ordered logically to take children from the basics of letter formation, through to phonics, understanding the structure of full sentences, and basic story comprehension. Material should ideally be followed in the order in which it is presented for a progressive development of skills.

★ HELP:

As you progress through the workbook with your child, help them by reading instructions aloud and explaining activities further.

★ ANSWERS:

Refer to the answers section at the back of the workbook once your child has completed an activity. Ensure they fully comprehend the concept presented before moving on to the next activity.

⭐ WRITING INSTRUMENT AND GRASP:

By kindergarten age, your child is getting comfortable using a pencil as their hand muscles and fine motor skills are developing. It is helpful, however, to frequently reinforce ideal pencil grasp, per the following steps:

We love reading and writing in **Happy Town**!

- Hold the pencil between thumb and index finger, with index finger on top.

- Rest the pencil on the middle finger.

- Rest the side of the hand comfortably on the table.

⭐ FORMATION:

This workbook uses a system of dots and numbered arrows to demonstrate the correct formation of letters.

- ● The black dot indicates the starting point for the pencil.

- → The arrows show the direction of pencil movement, and should be followed in numerical order.

- ◎ This additional dot indicates that the pencil should lift off the page to make a separate stroke.

⭐ WRITING LINES:

This workbook uses writing lines consisting of three lines with a dotted center to encourage proper character formation.

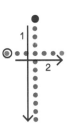

Building a Sentence

⭐ UPPERCASE LETTERS:

"A" is an uppercase letter and "a" is a lowercase letter.

How do you know when to use an uppercase letter?

You need to use one...

...at the beginning of a sentence:

What is this place called?

...for place names:

It is called Happy Town!

...for personal names:

King and Queen live in Happy Town!

...for "I":

I am called Prince.

...for days of the week:

Monday

Tuesday

Wednesday

Thursday

Friday

Saturday

Sunday

...for months of the year:

January

February

March

April

May

June

July

August

September

October

November

December

Circle what **day** it is today.

Circle the **month** in which your birthday falls.

What makes up a sentence?
A group of **words**, with **spaces** in between, and **punctuation**.

Look at the parts of this sentence:

word → **Happy** Town is a ← space

magical place where

everyone loves to laugh, ← comma

learn, and play! ← exclamation mark

Would you like to visit? ← question mark

Let's take a trip and ← apostrophe

see who we meet. ← period

9

Letters

Trace the letters. Then, fill in the **missing letters** in each sentence.

Aa
Bb

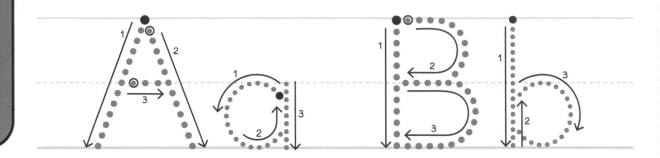

Alligator
likes apples.

Bee reads
a book.

Remember to form your **letters** carefully!

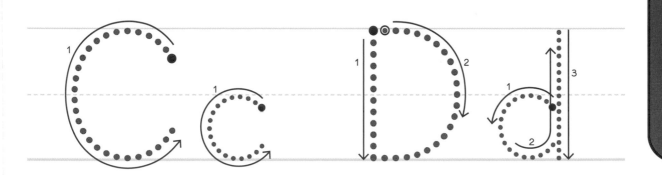

Cat is in
the car.

Dog digs in
the dirt.

Wow!
Great work.

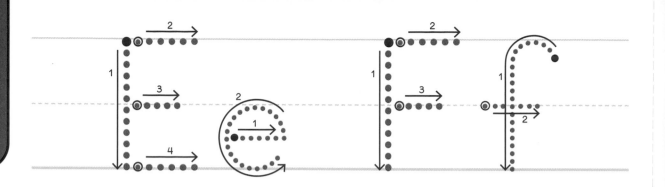

Elephant
eats eggs.

Frog lives on
a farm.

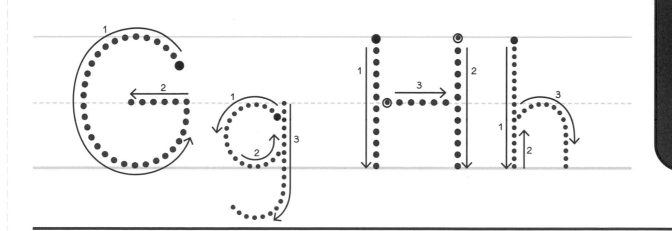

Goat likes to eat grass.

Hippo is happy.

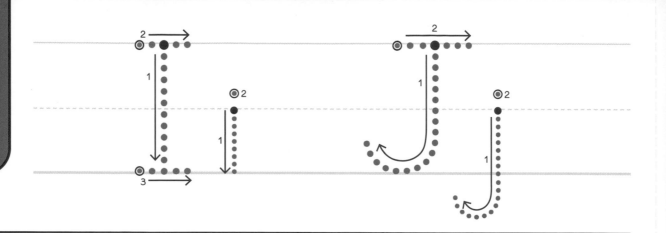

I guana sees an i gloo.

J aguar is in the j ungle.

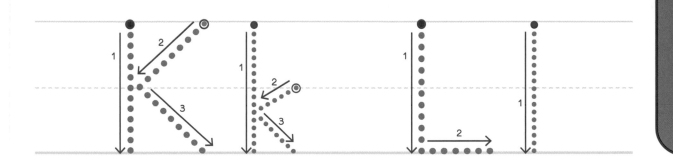

Kangaroo
is kind.

Lion is in the
library.

M m N n

Mouse makes magic!

Newt eats noodles.

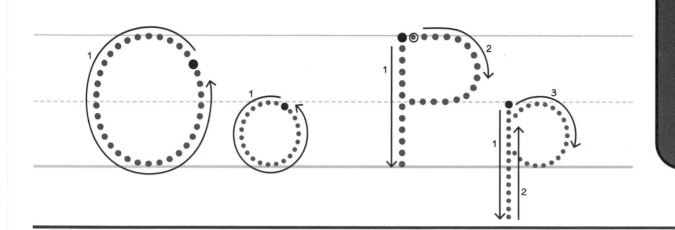

Octopus likes oranges.

Pig and Penguin play.

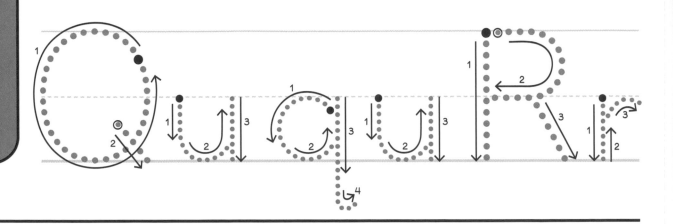

Queen asks questions.

Why do we learn **Qu/qu** together and not just **Qq**? It is because these letters almost always appear alongside one another!

Rabbit rides a roller coaster.

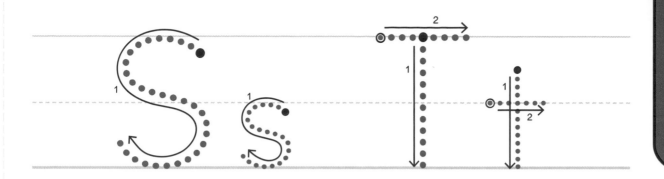

Snail has fun in the sun.

Tiger goes to town.

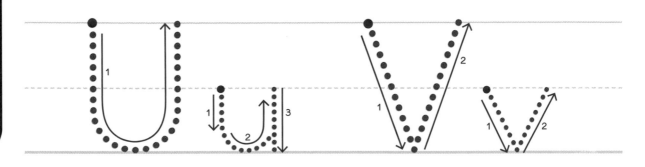

Unicorn has an
mbrella.

Vulture likes
egetables.

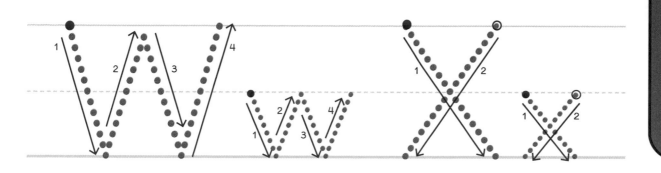

Walrus is in the wagon.

This is an X-ray fish.

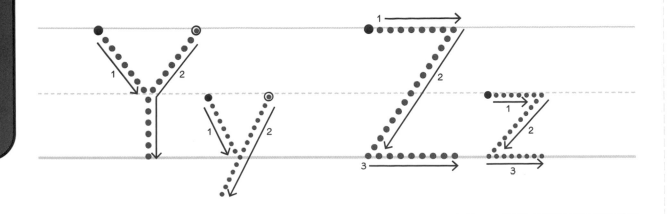

Yak can do yoga.

Zebra lives in the zoo.

Beginning Sounds

Circle the **beginning sound** of each picture.

(a) c n

e b d

i j d

b e f

p h l

o c x

k f l

m h n

b p o

q s r

g w h

t y z

Middle Sounds

Draw lines to match the picture with the correct **middle vowel sound** and word. Complete the words by writing the correct vowel.

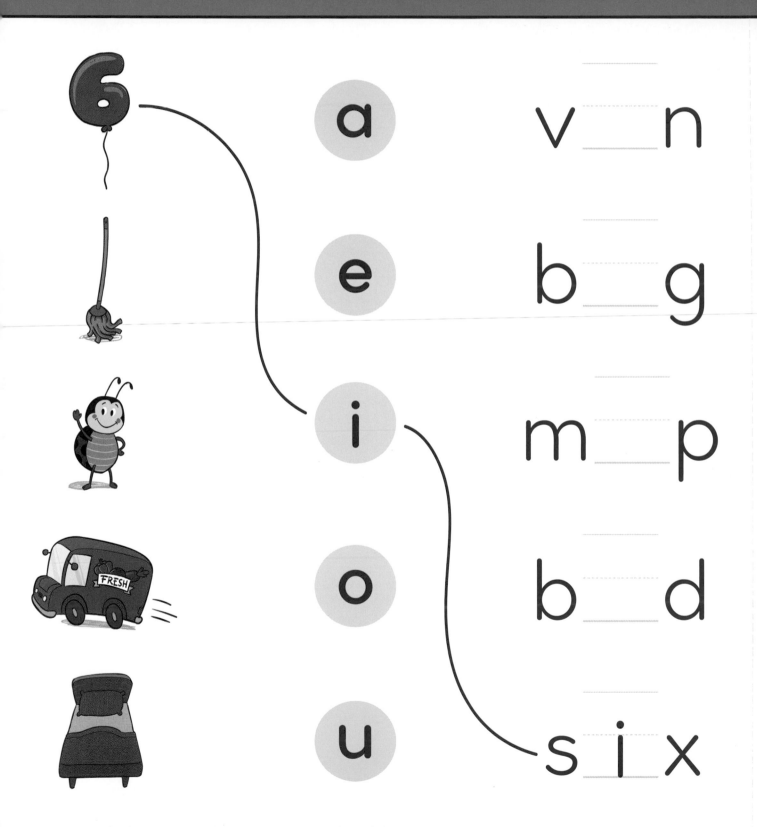

v _ n

b _ g

m _ p

b _ d

s _i_ x

 **a** l _ g

 **e** b _ s

 **i** y _ k

 **o** n _ t

 **u** f _ n

Vowel Sound Quiz

Write the missing **vowel sound** in the middle of each word.

a e i o u

c a t

h __ n

The **letters** in the key can be used more than once!

j __ m

l __ g

k __ d

h __ g

b __ x

c __ n

m __ d

p __ g

End Sounds

Circle the letter that is at the **end** of the word.

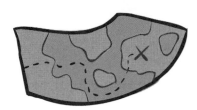

z a (p)

b t c

n d e

q s g

n k m

o p s

Write the letter that goes at the **end** of the word.

 ~~d~~ t b g x t

 b e d

 b u ___

 b a ___

 c u ___

 j e ___

 f o ___

Word Scramble

Write the letters in the correct **order** to spell the word.

e w b

_____

_____

a n p

_____

_____

n s u

_____

_____

h t a

_____

_____

Build a Word

Link the correct letters together and **write** the word.

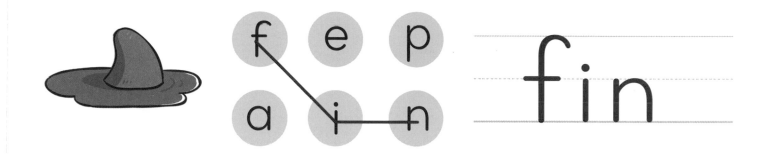

f e p

a i n

fin

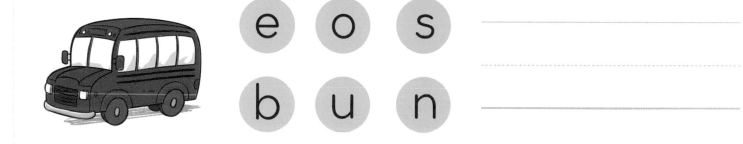

e o s

b u n

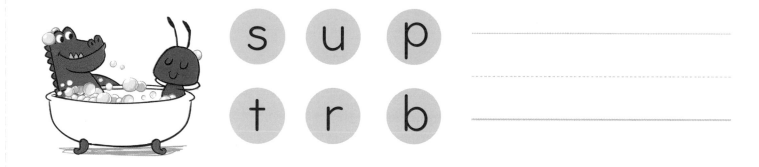

s u p

t r b

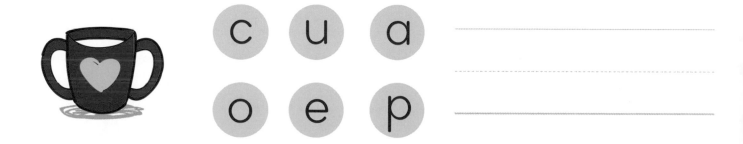

c u a

o e p

Word Match

(bag)

wag

tag

red

bed

ted

pig

big

dig

rug

bug

hug

fox

ox

box

rub

tub

cub

bat

cat

mat

jam

ham

ram

leg

peg

beg

zip

sip

lip

up

pup

cup

fun

sun

run

Rhyming Words

 cat

 dig

 hen

box

 pig

pan

 fox

pen

 van

log

 dog

rat

 bun

hop

 sad

jam

 ram

wet

 map

nap

 vet

mad

 cop

run

Beginning Blends

Fill in the blanks at the beginning of each word with the correct **letter blend** from the options below.

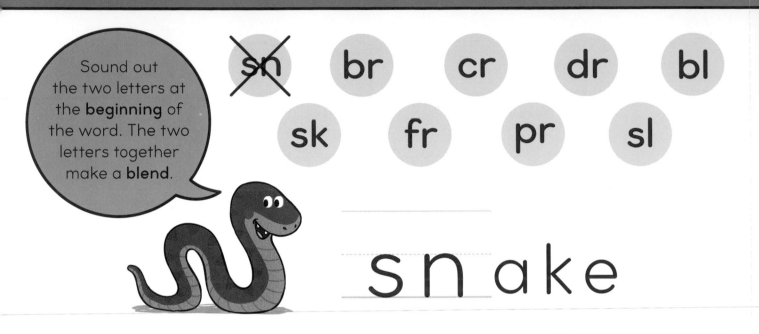

~~sn~~ br cr dr bl

sk fr pr sl

Sound out the two letters at the **beginning** of the word. The two letters together make a **blend**.

_____

s n a k e

_____

u g

_____

u n k

_____

_____

o g

 _____ oc

 _____ ide

 _____ imp

_____ one

 _____ ince

Ending Blends

Fill in the blanks at the end of each word with the correct **letter blend** from the options below.

 ~~ing~~ ift elp ump and

ilt ent est ilk

Sound out the letters at the **end** of the word. The letters together make a **blend**.

king

h _____

t _____

m _____

n _____

j _____

qu _____

g _____

h _____

Digraphs

Fill in the blanks with the correct **sound** at the **beginning** or **end** of these words.

ch wh sh th ph ck qu

Digraphs are **two letters** that make **one sound!**

bea ch

_____ ark

_____ one

____ ree

du ____

____ een

____ ale

Digraphs

Draw lines to match each word with the **sound** it contains.

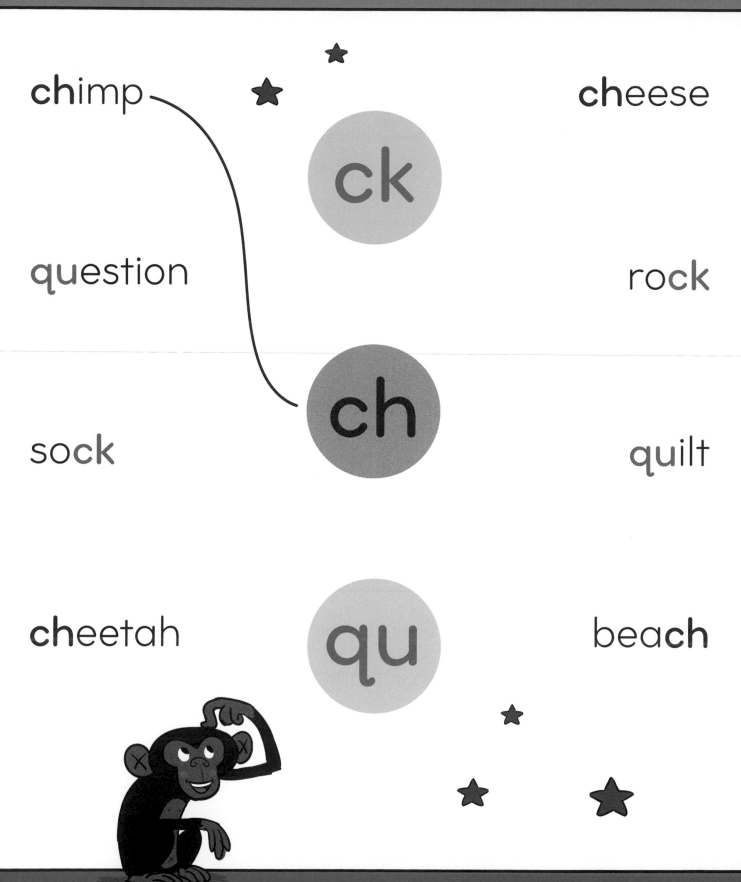

chimp

cheese

ck

question

rock

ch

so**ck**

quilt

cheetah

qu

bea**ch**

wheel

white

whiskers

shirt

sh

wi**sh**

think

ph

ba**th**

shell

sheep

photo

th

ele**ph**ant

wh

throw

Sight Word Match

Draw lines to pair the matching **sight words**.

Sight Word Search

Find and circle the **sight words** in the word search.

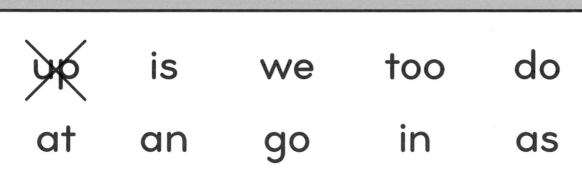

up   is   we   too   do

at   an   go   in   as

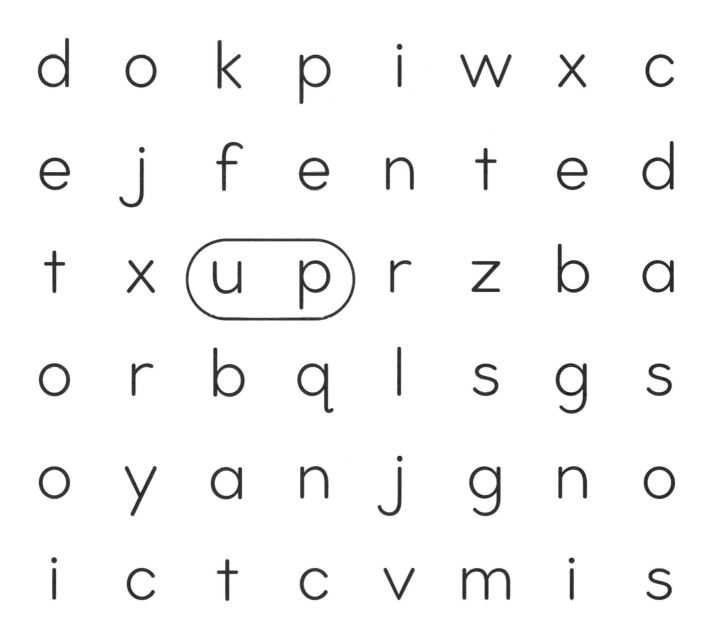

d o k p i w x c

e j f e n t e d

t x (u p) r z b a

o r b q l s g s

o y a n j g n o

i c t c v m i s

Sight Word Practice

Trace the **sight words** to complete the sentence.

Unicorn _is up_ _on a_ unicycle.

Yum! _I_ love cake.

_Do we_ all love cake?

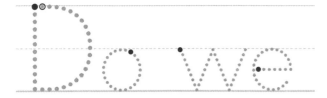

I love cookies _too_ !

Turtle and Tiger

go to town.

Cat is in the car at the market.

Iguana lives

on an island.

Sight Word Practice

Circle the correct **sight words** to complete each sentence.

(**It**)   **To**   **on**   (**is**)   a kite, high

(**in**)   **a**   the sky.

Bee reads

of   **a**   book

to   **an**   Bear.

Fly lives

on   **to**

as   **a**

flower.

Elephant | **is** | **too** |

| **do** | **so** | big!

Is Mouse | **go** | **as** | big

| **as** | **we** | Elephant?

| **No,** | **Up,** | Mouse | **I** | **is** | not

| **as** | **at** | big.

Color by Sight Word

Color the picture according to the **sight word** key.

● am ● me ● my ● the ● for

● and ● be ● by ● big ○ all

52

Sight Word Scramble

Unscramble the **sight words** and match them to the correct spelling.

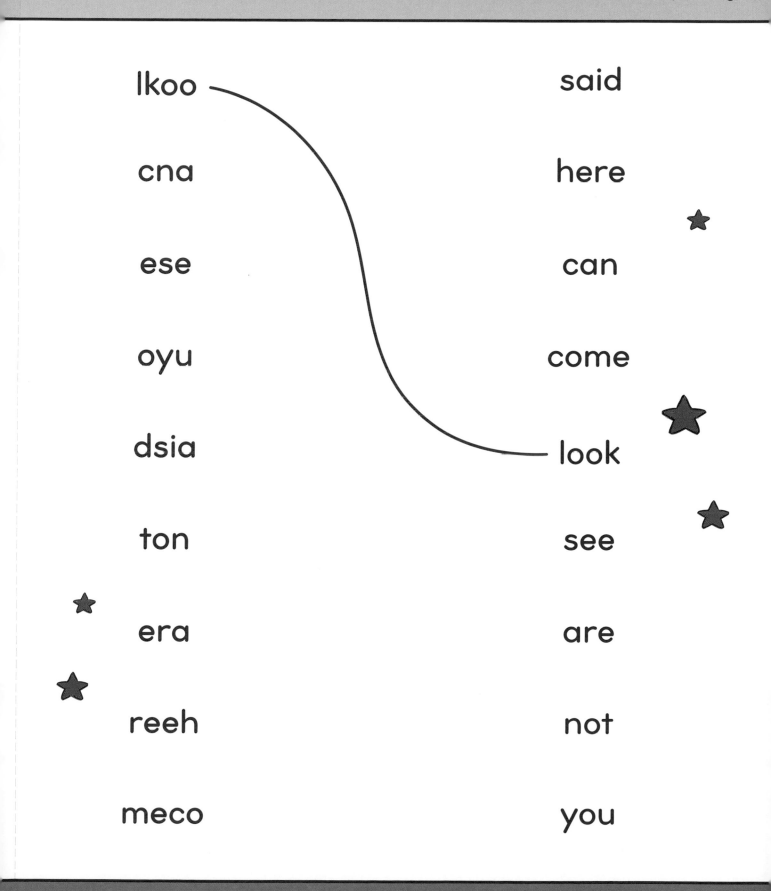

lkoo	said
cna	here
ese	can
oyu	come
dsia	look
ton	see
era	are
reeh	not
meco	you

Sight Word Practice

Complete the sentences by using the **sight words** provided on each page.

~~I~~   ~~am~~   big   and   me   My   is

I am _____ Yeti.

Yetis are _____

_____ strong.

Have you met _____ yet?

_____ name

_____ Bess.

I   be   of   in   like   we   the   all

Can _____ _____ your friend?

All _____ us are friends

_____ Happy Town!

If you _____ , _____

can play in _____

park _____ day!

Sight Word Practice

Complete the sentences by using the **sight words** provided on each page.

for	can	see	you	said

King and
Queen look

_____

_____ Duck.

"I _____ _____

_____ , Duck!"

_____ Queen.

not   here   are   Come   said

The truck will _____ budge.

It is stuck _____ !

Fly's friends

_____

at the beach.

" _____ to the city!"

_____ Cat.

Color Sight Words

Trace the **color sight words** to complete each sentence.

The jam is

red.

Elephant is

blue.

The cab is

yellow.

Frog is

green.

Tiger is

orange.

Octopus is

purple.

Pig is

pink.

Dog is

brown.

Word Fill

Write the **missing letters** in these words.

n   qu   s   i   o   t

elephan

lio

guana

ctopus

een

kunk

Word Scramble

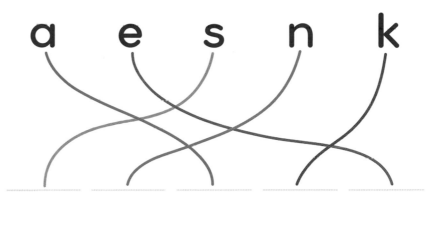

a   e   s   n   k

g   o   r   f

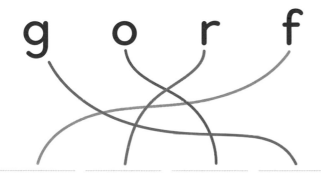

e   t   n   w

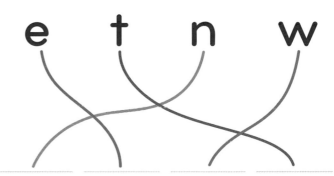

Syllables

Say the name of each character and circle the correct number of beats, or **syllables**, it contains.

Alligator

A syllable is like a **beat**. Clap your hands as you say the word to help you count the beats!

1 2 3 4

Elephant

1 2 3 4

Kangaroo

1 2 3 4

Octopus

1 2 3 4

Cat

1 2 3 4

Lion

1 2 3 4

Case Quiz

Uppercase or **lowercase**? Write the correct option for each word.

B **b**

____ e d

B **b**

____ o b

H **h**

____ a t

N **n**

____ e t

C **c**

____ u p

P **p**

____ e n

H h

___ appy

T t

___ own

T t

___ ed

L l

___ eg

M m

___ ap

V v

___ an

Sentence Scramble

Unscramble the words and write each **sentence** correctly.

Hint! Punctuation goes at the end of the sentence.

Happy / is / fun! / Town

Dog / Happy / Town. / in / lives

plays / Dog / dirt. / in / the

Dog / dirt. / digs / the / in

digs / Dog / dinosaur /
bone! / up / a

Sentence Fill

sun   hot   beach   book

Remember to use an **uppercase** letter at the beginning of a sentence!

The _____ is out. It is _____!

Duck goes to the

.

Lion reads a

.

Ant   Hen   camp   Frog   hop   Hen   nest

_____ and _____

go to _____ .

_____ likes _____ in the

_____ to _____ pond!

sits in

_____ her _____ .

69

Asking Questions

Sometimes we ask **questions**. A question always has a **question mark**. Look at the pictures and read the questions. Draw a line to the answer to each question.

Questions:

What does Elephant have?

Who can have an apple?

Answers:

Alligator can have an apple.

Elephant has a red pen.

Questions:

When does Fox go to his den to sleep?

Where is my quilt?

Why do Ant and Alligator go to the Snack Shack?

How does Cat get to the city?

Answers:

In a car!

When the sun comes up.

They go to buy snacks!

Here it is!

Pig's Busy Day

Describe what is happening in the **story**.

- Who is the main character in the story?

- How does Pig feel at the start?

- How does Pig feel at the end?

- Why is the truck stuck?

- How would you feel if you were Pig?

- What do you think happens next?

More Sight Words

Here are some more **sight words** to add to your vocabulary.
Learn a new word, create a sentence using it, and check it off!

after ☐	every ☐	her ☐
again ☐	find ☐	him ☐
any ☐	four ☐	his ☐
ask ☐	from ☐	how ☐
ate ☐	funny ☐	into ☐
away ☐	get ☐	jump ☐
black ☐	give ☐	just ☐
brown ☐	going ☐	know ☐
but ☐	good ☐	let ☐
came ☐	had ☐	little ☐
could ☐	has ☐	live ☐
did ☐	have ☐	make ☐
down ☐	he ☐	may ☐
eat ☐	help ☐	must ☐

new ☐	saw ☐	under ☐
now ☐	★ say ☐	walk ☐
old ☐	she ☐	want ☐
once ☐	some ☐	was ☐
one ☐	soon ☐	well ☐
open ☐	stop ☐	went ☐
our ☐	take ☐	were ☐
★ out ☐	thank ☐	what ☐
★ over ☐	that ☐	when ☐
play ☐	them ☐	where ☐
please ☐	then ☐	★ white ☐
pretty ☐	there ☐	who ☐
put ☐	they ☐	★ will ☐
ran ☐	think ☐	with ☐
ride ☐	this ☐	yes ☐
round ☐	three ☐	
run ☐	two ☐	

Answers

PHONICS

Page 23:
bee: **b**
dog: **d**
egg: **e**

Page 24:
pan: **p**
cup: **c**
fox: **f**
hat: **h**

Page 25:
bag: **b**
sun: **s**
web: **w**
zoo: **z**

Pages 26-27:

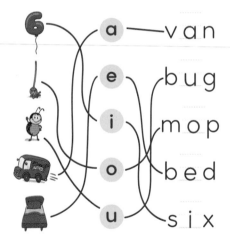

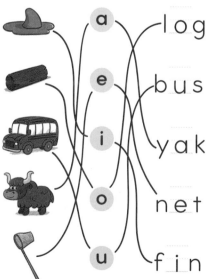

Page 28:
hen
jam
leg

Page 29:
kid
hog
box
can
mud
pig

Page 30:
net: **t**
pen: **n**
log: **g**
yak: **k**
bus: **s**

Page 31:
bug
bat
cub
jet
fox

Page 32:
web
pan
sun
hat

Page 33:

  bus

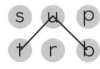 tub

 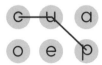 cup

Page 34:
bed
dig
bug
fox
cub

Page 35:
cat
ram
leg
sip
up
sun

Page 36:
hen and **pen**
pig and **dig**
fox and **box**
van and **pan**
dog and **log**

Page 37:
bun and **run**
sad and **mad**
ram and **jam**
map and **nap**
vet and **wet**
cop and **hop**

Page 38:
slug
skunk
frog

Page 39:
croc
bride
blimp
drone
prince

Page 40:
help
tent

Page 41:
milk
nest
jump
quilt
gift
hand

Page 42:
shark
phone

Page 43:
three
duck
queen
whale

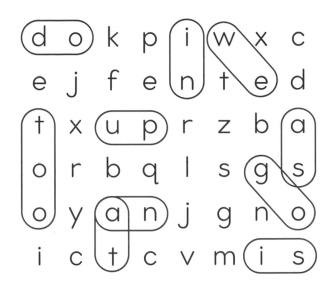

Page 44:
ck: sock; rock
ch: cheese; beach; cheetah
qu: question; quilt

Page 45:
sh: wish; sheep; shirt; shell
ph: elephant; photo
th: bath; think; throw
wh: wheel; whiskers; white

SIGHT WORDS
Page 46:

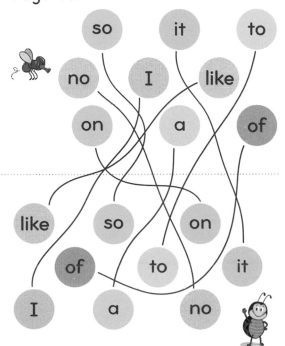

so   it   to
no   I   like
on   a   of

like   so   on
of   to   it
I   a   no

Page 47:

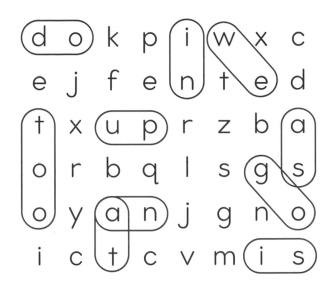

Page 50:
Bee reads **a** book **to** Bear.
Fly lives **on a** flower.

Page 51:
Elephant **is so** big!
Is Mouse **as** big **as** Elephant?
No, Mouse **is** not **as** big.

Page 52:

Page 53:

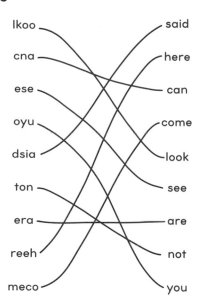

lkoo — look
cna — can
ese — see
oyu — you
dsia — said
ton — not
era — are
reeh — here
meco — come

Page 54:
Yetis are **big and** strong.
Have you met **me** yet?
My name **is** Bess.

Page 55:
Can **I be** your friend?
All **of** us are friends **in** Happy Town!
If you **like**, **we** can play in **the** park **all** day!

Page 56:
King and Queen look **for** Duck.
"I **can see you**, Duck!" **said** Queen.

Page 57:
The truck will **not** budge. It is stuck **here**!
Fly's friends **are** at the beach.
"**Come** to the city!" **said** Cat.

WORD WORK

Page 60:
elephant
lion
iguana
octopus
queen
skunk

Page 61:
snake
frog
newt

Page 62:
Alligator: **4**
Elephant: **3**

Page 63:
Kangaroo: **3**
Octopus: **3**
Cat: **1**
Lion: **2**

Page 64:
bed
Bob
hat
net
cup
pen

Page 65:
Happy Town
Ted
leg
map
van

Page 66:
Happy Town is fun!
Dog lives in Happy Town.

Page 67:
Dog plays in the dirt.
Dog digs in the dirt.
Dog digs up a dinosaur bone!

Page 68:
The **sun** is out. It is **hot**!
Duck goes to the **beach**.
Lion reads a **book**.

Page 69:
Ant and **Hen** go to **camp**.
Frog likes to **hop** in the pond!
Hen sits in her **nest**.

COMPREHENSION

Page 70:
Who can have an apple?
Alligator can have an apple.

When does Fox go to his den to sleep?
When the sun comes up.

Where is my quilt? **Here it is!**

Why do Ant and Alligator go to the Snack Shack? **They go to buy snacks!**

How does Cat get to the city? **In a car!**

Certificate

This certificate is awarded to:

for learning reading and writing skills!

Age: _____ Date: _____

Signed: _____

THE READING HOUSE